Vidalia® Onion Store
Recipe Book

1993 Edition

Vidalia® Onion is a registered trademark of the Georgia Department of Agriculture.

The Vidalia Onion Store
P.O. Box 1719
Vidalia, GA 30474

Text: Viki Brigham
Editor: Linda M. Sciullo
Production: Carol L. Parrott

First printing March 1993

ISBN #0-915099-48-9

Contents

Main Dish...............................36

Side Dishes 52

Breads &
Miscellaneous 60

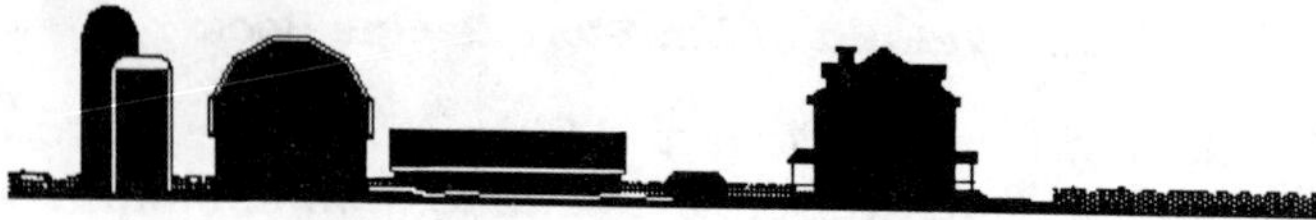

FARMER GRIMES

In spring when a man's fancy is suppose to turn to love, W.J. Grimes' fancy turns to onions.

In fairness, however, his mind and his heart rarely stray far from onions. "'Round here, we're thinking about onions all the time," he says. And Grimes, his family and friends don't just think, talk, plant, eat and dream about any old onion. It's the very special — some might say golden — Vidalia® Onion. Beginning near the end of April, the "dirt will be cracking all around" this special onion and that signals the beginning of the harvest, which will continue until the middle of June.

At the height of the season, there will be more than 200 workers dragging croker sacks (burlap bags) up and down the rows of the 500-acre Grimes' farm. W.J. Grimes, one of Southeast Georgia's premier onion growers, planted those rows with the yellow granex hybrid known for its sweet, mild flavor.

Covered with golden onion skin, the Vidalia Onion has also proved to be golden in many ways for the growers in the 20-county area centered around the Southeast Georgia town of Vidalia. The distinctive onions take their name from the rural community, though there are no farms actually in Vidalia.

Back in 1976, Grimes recalls, "You couldn't hardly make a living farming corn and beans." Still, Grimes closed down his grain and livestock operations to concentrate on vegetables, particularly black-eyed peas, collards and onions. That was before he got into Vidalia Onions in a big way, back when the black-eyed peas were lots more important than the onions. Grimes tells a story about "chipping up some of those New Jersey onions on my black-eyed peas and darn near ruining 'em, the peas, that is."

He laughs and adds, "We've learned a lot about onions since then. But we got a lot more to learn."

Grimes and the golden Vidalia Onion didn't get into the big time until the 1980s, but the Vidalia Onion made an unassuming debut back during the Depression when a man named Mose Coleman discovered that the onions he'd planted were sweet instead of hot. Coleman dragged his croker sacks from store to store in Toombs County, Grimes says, where the sweet hybrid "went over real big."

Soon other farmers followed suit, but the distinctive onion was still only known locally. In those days, according to a Vidalia Onion Association publication, Coleman and his colleagues were delighted when a 50-pound sack of onions sold for $3.50.

The Vidalia Onion has been analyzed inside and out by premier scientists at some of the most prestigious universities in the country, but the cause of its sweet taste remains as mysterious as it was when Coleman bit into that first one. "If we knew why these onions are sweet instead of hot, we'd all be millionaires," says Grace Manning, a local farmer.

The sweet onion appears to be a unique and fortunate blending of a yellow granex hybrid with the soil. "The soil has funny little rocks in it," says Grimes. Those whose knowledge of Georgia begins and ends with Atlanta are often surprised to hear that the unique soil around Vidalia is loamy and not red like that of middle Georgia. That soil plus the particular seed and the mild winters and early springs combine to produce the sweet Vidalia Onion that can't be replicated anyplace else in the United States.

In the 1940s, the state built a farmers' market in Vidalia, not because of the onions, but because of the blacktop: Vidalia was at the juncture of some of South

Georgia's busiest highways, including the one from the North that carried tourists to Florida. Soon, the market, which featured the distinctive sweet onion, was doing a brisk business among the tourists.

Then came the 1950s. As Grimes tells it, there was a small grocery chain in the area that was floundering, and its far-flung owners sent a young man to the Vidalia area to close down the stores and sell off the assets.

Instead, he got caught up in marketing the unique golden onion. Between his marketing and the tourists stopping by to inquire about "that onion from Vidalia," it wasn't long before the Vidalia Onion's reputation spread across the United States.

"And the rest, as they say, is history," says Grimes with a laugh.

Controlled Atmosphere Storage

The W.J. Grimes family has been farming in Southeast Georgia for more than a hundred years, but it wasn't until Mose Coleman noticed that the onions he'd planted tasted sweet instead of hot that Grimes and his fellow onion growers tasted success.

Several years ago, it occurred to Grimes and some of his grower friends that if they could store onions for long periods of time, the season could be extended weeks, months, even year-round.

Working with Dr. Doyle Smittle, horticulture researcher with the University of Georgia Agriculture Experiment Station in Tifton, Georgia, and with other nationally known university scientists, the Vidalia Onion Committee, of which Grimes is a three times past president, came up with Controlled Atmosphere. C.A. (Controlled Atmosphere) storage is envisioned to do for the onion what similar technology has done for the apple, according to Grimes.

The growers spent months and thousands of dollars building huge storage rooms that could be climate-controlled. Grimes predicted that the onion farmers would be capable of increasing their plantings from 5,500 acres to an estimated 18,000 acres using C.A. storage to handle the surplus onions.

"What we were trying to do was to get the onions to go back to sleep for a while instead of sprouting," says Grimes.

According to Smittle, the onion farmers try to sell all of their crop during the six-week harvest period. In a good year, that means the market is glutted and everyone loses money.

"Now, we are looking at the possibility of marketing Vidalia Onions over six months," says Smittle. He theorized that the Vidalia Onion would hold up well when the humidity is 70-75 percent, the temperature is 34-35 degrees, and the atmosphere is constant at 3 percent oxygen, 5 percent carbon dioxide and 92 percent nitrogen. Translating that into action, Grimes stuffed his 80,000-square-foot C.A. storage area with tons of onions, and he waited.

The first batch of onions, says Grimes, came out tasting better than when they went in. "I feel certain the future for Vidalia Onion production rests in C.A. storage," he said during the press conference that followed the opening of the first C.A. storage bins.

Now, several years later, the few kinks have been straightened out so that the C.A. onions meet the same stringent criteria that Grimes sets for all his onions. What that means for Vidalia Onion lovers, Grimes says with a grin, is "onion heaven on earth" six months of the year.

And they're good for you!

If an apple a day will keep the doctor away, an onion

a day will probably keep you away from the doctor, the nurse and the nutritionist.

According to recent reports from the National Cancer Institute, onions are the latest weapon in the cancer-fighting arsenal. The onion is thought to lower the risk of stomach cancer, Institute scientists say.

Not only that, but chemists at East Texas State University have isolated a chemical in onions that has the ability to lower blood pressure. The natural chemical is prostaglandin A1.

Studies also show that eating onions can reduce cholesterol levels in the blood and help stop dangerous clotting.

But you don't have to be ill or at-risk to benefit from eating your onions:

* A Vidalia Onion has twice the vitamin C of an apple
* A Vidalia Onion has as much vitamin C as an orange
* A medium-sized Vidalia Onion has 2.8 grams of dietary fiber

Vidalia Onions have zero fat and cholesterol and only 60 calories per serving. While a medium-sized onion has little sodium — 10 mg — it has lots of potassium — 200 mg, in fact.

A Vidalia Onion provides one gram of protein, which is half the daily requirement as established by the U.S. RDA. It also provides 14 grams of carbohydrates.

They'll fight to protect the Vidalia Onion

Why will growers fight to protect the Vidalia Onion? Because it's the sweetest onion in the country. It is gourmet. It is to onions what Grade A tenderloin is to a cow — the choicest and the best available.

In 1978, the Vidalia Onion Association was formed to promote the product, and in 1979 several growers "got on a television show and got us a little publicity," says W.J. Grimes. The cause was also helped by enterprising growers who sponsor and promote area onion festivals, which are an annual event in both Vidalia and nearby Glennville.

But, it wasn't long before growers from outside the area tried to horn in on the onion phenomenon by labeling their onions "Vidalias." To promote the true Vidalia Onion, the Georgia legislature passed a bill in 1986 establishing the Vidalia Onion's legal status and defining the 20-county production area. That was capped off in 1988 when the producers united to establish a Federal Marketing Order for the crop, which extends the definition of a Vidalia Onion to the federal level.

Later, the Vidalia Onion was named Georgia's official state vegetable.

According to the Vidalia Onion Association, some 250 growers cultivate the prized onions on about 5,500 acres. The average grower plants 22 acres with a yield of 300 50-pound bags to the acre. The small-scale growers are most apt to sell their products to small-market operations or at roadside produce markets. Even though the interstate system bypasses Vidalia, savvy tourists travel miles out of their way to snag a bag of the genuine item.

The remaining 70 percent of the harvest is gobbled up by big grocery chains and mail-order businesses.

The Vidalia Onion costs a bit more than ordinary onions and for a good reason. From seed to kitchen, it's mostly done by hand. When the onion is ready to be harvested, the laborers driving the big machinery take their blades and carefully run them under the onions. Then the workers with the croker sacks walk the fields, snipping off the tops and placing the onions in the sacks. If the weather cooperates — no rain in the forecast — the bags are left in the field for several days so the onions can dry. "They're tender and green when they're picked," says Grimes. "They have to turn golden brown with a crusty layer" before they're ready to be sorted, he says.

Once in the huge warehouse, the onions are stored in gigantic hoppers with gas heaters that dry them further. Then they are placed on conveyer belts with holes in them. The jumbos stay on the top belt, while the mediums drop down to the next belt and the peewees to the lowest belt. All of the belts are lined with rubber so the onions won't bruise. That's because one bruised onion — like the proverbial bad apple — will spoil the sack.

One of Grimes' workers comments that the boss is an easy-going fellow until he sees someone handling the onions "roughly."

"Most of the damage (to onions) is from rough handling. You have to handle them like eggs," Grimes says. Grimes learned a long time ago that the first rule of successful merchandising is to offer a superior product. "We only keep the best ones. We throw the others away," he says. "I won't even give the culls away. I dig a big ditch and bury them." Some 20 percent of every year's crop ends up in that ditch.

How to handle a Vidalia Onion

A Vidalia Onion must be handled gently, like an apple or an egg. Don't toss your Vidalia Onions into a basket or box, for example, because if one of them is bruised and begins to rot, it could spread to the others.

The best way to preserve your Vidalia Onions is to keep them dry, separate and cool.

You may store your onions in the legs of old, clean, sheer pantyhose. Tie a knot between each onion and cut below the knot when you want an onion. Hang in a cool, dry, well-ventilated area. There are also onion hangers available from The Vidalia Onion Store that are similar to pantyhose storage.

Some consumers simply spread their onions on racks or screens. Make sure the onions do not touch each other and store in a cool place.

Onions can be frozen. Chop the onions and spread them on cookie sheets. Place the cookie sheets in the freezer. When frozen, remove and place in freezer containers or plastic bags. Seal containers or bags and put them back in the freezer. This method allows the cook to remove only as many as she needs.

Some freeze whole, jumbo Vidalia Onions by peeling, washing, coring and dropping them into plastic bags. Once frozen, they may be removed like ice cubes.

Caution: Freezing changes the texture of the onions, so frozen onions should only be used for cooking.

Onions forever

It seems that onions always have been and always will be a food fact. According to historians, the onion is the most common vegetable in the world — no cuisine is without them — and has been around in one form or another for 6,000 years.

Most people take onions for granted, but would miss them, were they to disappear. "It's hard to imagine a civilization without onions; in one form or another, their flavor blends into almost everything in the meal except dessert," writes Julia Child in *Mastering the Art of French Cooking.*

Onions have been cultivated for so long that no one knows precisely when or where they originated. Some say onions have been grown in China, India and the Middle

East since prehistoric times.

Onions were a well-known vegetable in Egypt. In fact, evidence of their existence dates from books of the second dynasties (3200 - 2780 B.C.) Not only were onions eaten, they were sculptured on ancient Egyptian monuments and were present in the worship and daily lives of the people. There is even evidence that onions were so highly regarded that they became symbols of morality or ethics. Onions were used for swearing oaths, in much the same way we use the Bible.

Onions flourished in ancient Egypt among the pyramid laborers, who ate them and their first cousin, garlic, to ward off illness and prevent fatigue.

The Israelites thought so highly of onions that they cultivated them in Palestine after the Exodus, about 1500 B.C.

The Romans, who also gave the world paved roads, law and plumbing, introduced onions to the inhabitants of both the British Isles and Western Europe. They were considered so valuable that they were often used for currency during the Middle Ages.

Early on, the Spanish brought the onion to the New World where it quickly spread to all parts of the Americas, even though Native Americans were already using a variety of wild onion to flavor their food.

Onion tidbits

* One pound of small onions will serve three or four people.
* To remove onion flavor from your hands, wash them in cold water, rub them with salt, rinse them again in cold water, and then wash in soap and warm water.
* Onions add subtlety to a dish.
* A tablespoon of freshly chopped onion added to canned vegetables often disguises the "canned" taste and varies the expected flavor.
* If you scorch onions, they will taste bitter.
* High heat and long cooking bring out the worst features of onions.
* If you want mild onion flavor with little onion odor, blanch the onions for several minutes before adding them to soups or stews.
* Sauté onions only until translucent and tender for mild onion flavor.
* For penetrating onion flavor, sauté until golden, and for dominant onion flavor, brown onions very slowly.
* To shorten cooking time, chop onions very finely.
* Chopping is easier and safer if you first slice a flat base in the onion and use a sharp knife.
* If you don't have time to chop and sauté, use a food processor.
* Eating raw parsley freshens onion breath.
* Onions deteriorate rapidly once the outer skin is removed.

🥣 Appetizers 🥣

Sausage-Stuffed Onion Appetizers

12-14 small Vidalia Onions (about 3 inches
  in diameter)
1 pound sausage
1 clove of garlic, minced
1 tablespoon olive oil
1/4 cup fresh parsley, chopped

Peel onions and simmer, covered, in small amount of boiling water for 15 minutes. Drain and cool until you can handle them. Hollow out centers by pushing hard on bottoms or pulling them out with a small, sharp knife or grapefruit knife.

Finely chop centers. Sauté in olive oil with sausage and garlic, stirring to crumble up sausage.

Cook about 10 minutes or until sausage is well-browned and onion and garlic are limp and tender. Drain off all fat and add parsley.

With a small spoon, carefully fill onion shells. Arrange in shallow baking dish, just large enough to hold them. Add 1 inch hot water.

Cover with aluminum foil and bake in preheated 375-degree oven for 30 minutes.

Cool and refrigerate. Remove from refrigerator 1 hour before serving. (12 servings)

Vidalia Onion Dip

This recipe separates the casual onion user from the onion addict.

1 medium Vidalia Onion, finely chopped
1 small can (2 1/4 ounce) chopped black olives,
  (about 4 tablespoons)
4 tablespoons olive oil
1 tablespoon wine vinegar
1 teaspoon Worcestershire sauce
1 4-ounce can chopped green chili peppers
1 large tomato, finely chopped
1/4 cup fresh parsley, finely chopped
dash of Tabasco sauce
salt and pepper to taste

Combine all ingredients and chill well. Taste and adjust seasonings. Serve with corn chips, crackers or pita bread.

Vidalia Onion Beef Dip

1 jar dried beef, finely chopped
1 medium Vidalia Onion, finely chopped
1/2 cup sour cream
1/2 teaspoon freshly ground black pepper
1 clove garlic, mashed
1 8-ounce package cream cheese, softened
1/2 cup pecans, chopped

Beat cream cheese until soft and creamy. Add other ingredients, except nuts, and blend well. Spread in baking dish and sprinkle with nuts.

Bake in a preheated 350-degree oven for about 6 minutes.

Note: This dip may also be served cold. After blending ingredients, shape into ball and roll in crushed nuts. Chill for several hours before serving with an assortment of crackers. This is inappropriate for a low-fat, low-cholesterol diet.

French Fried
Onion Rings

2 large Vidalia Onions
buttermilk
flour
1 teaspoon salt
1/4 teaspoon pepper
cooking oil

Slice onions and separate into rings. Cover with buttermilk and allow to stand for 1 hour. Place flour, salt and pepper in a plastic food-storage bag; add onion rings and shake to coat. Fry in hot oil (about 350 degrees on electric skillet setting). Drain on paper towels and serve warm. (serves 4)

Vidalia Onion Mold
With Crackers

1 cup pecans, chopped
1 medium Vidalia Onion, finely minced
1 pound sharp Cheddar cheese
2 cloves garlic, mashed
2/3 cup mayonnaise
1/2 teaspoon Tabasco sauce
1 1/3 cups strawberry preserves

Place cheese, onion, garlic, Tabasco and mayonnaise in food processor and process until smooth.

Remove from processor and fold in pecans. Pour into ring mold and chill.

Unmold on serving platter that has been covered with lettuce and fill center with preserves. Serve with assortment of crackers.

Note: Some of the fat may be cut from this recipe by substituting a light cheese for the cheddar and a soy-based mayonnaise for the more traditional egg mayonnaise.

Salads

Stuffed Vidalia Onion Salad

5 large Vidalia Onions
2 tablespoons deviled ham
1 tablespoon chopped pimento
1 8-ounce package cream cheese, softened
1 1/4 teaspoon dry mustard
1/8 teaspoon freshly ground black pepper

Peel onions. Remove centers and reserve for another recipe.

Beat cream cheese until it is soft and creamy. Blend in ham and remaining ingredients. Fill onion shells with mixture and chill several hours.

To serve, slice onions and place on lettuce leaves. (10 to 12 servings)

Optional: garnish with slice of fresh tomato and sprig of parsley.

Vidalia Onion and Cucumber Salad

1 medium cucumber, peeled and thinly sliced
1 medium onion, thinly sliced
1 medium tomato, chopped
1/4 cup parsley
salt and pepper
2 tablespoons olive oil
1 tablespoon vinegar
1 cup non-fat yogurt

Combine cucumber, onion, parsley and tomato in serving dish. Salt and pepper to taste. Mix olive oil and vinegar and pour over vegetables. Mix well. Add yogurt and mix well.

Turkey Salad Bake

2 cups crushed potato chips
4 tablespoons grated Vidalia Onion
1 cup shredded sharp cheddar cheese
1 tablespoon butter
1/2 cup chopped pecans
3 cups cooked, diced turkey
1 cup chopped celery
1/2 cup mayonnaise
lemon juice
salt and pepper to taste
Preheat oven to 350 degrees.

Combine cheese and potato chips; place half of the mixture in the bottom of a greased, shallow baking dish. Melt butter in small skillet over low heat. Add pecans and sauté until brown. Drain on paper towels.

Mix pecans with onions, turkey, celery, mayonnaise, lemon juice, salt and pepper. Pour into baking dish and cover with remaining potato chip mixture. Bake for 20 minutes. (6 servings)

Note: This recipe is inappropriate for those on a low-fat, low-cholesterol diet.

Red Cabbage Salad

4-6 cups red cabbage, coarsely chopped
1 medium Vidalia Onion, thinly sliced and
   separated into rings
1 small cucumber, peeled and sliced
2 fresh tomatoes, quartered
1/4 cup fresh parsley, chopped
2 tablespoons bleu cheese, crumbled
1 teaspoon McCormick's Salad
   Supreme Seasoning
salt and pepper to taste
Italian dressing
Place cabbage, onion, cucumber, tomatoes and pars-

ley in salad bowl and mix gently. Sprinkle bleu cheese and seasonings on top and dress with a commercial dressing or make your own. This salad is so versatile, almost any dressing tastes good. (6 servings)

Note: This is one of the few salads that will keep for several hours in the refrigerator after the dressing has been added. Also, if you leave off the bleu cheese and use a low-fat dressing, it is a tasty and colorful dish for those who are watching their cholesterol and fat intake.

Betsy's Summer Salad

1 bunch romaine lettuce
3-4 cups fresh strawberries, washed, hulled
    and sliced
2 medium Vidalia Onions, thinly sliced and
    separated into rings
1 cup walnuts, coarsely chopped

Dressing:
    1 1/2 cups sugar
    1/3 cup lemon juice
    1 teaspoon celery seed
    1 teaspoon dry mustard
    1 teaspoon paprika
    1/2 teaspoon salt
    3/4 cup salad oil (not olive)

Rinse lettuce under cold water and tear into bite-sized pieces. Place in large salad bowl. Add strawberries, onions and walnuts and mix well.

Mix sugar and lemon juice. Add celery seed, mustard, paprika and salt. Mix well. Whisk with wire whisk while slowly adding salad oil. Continue beating with whisk until the oil is incorporated. Pour over salad and toss well. (8 servings)

Note: This recipe is low in cholesterol, but it is somewhat high in its overall fat content. It is not appropriate for those on a low-fat or low-calorie diet.

Vicky's Potato Salad

6-9 medium potatoes, cooked, peeled and sliced
1 large carton cottage cheese
1 cup sour cream
2/3 cup mayonnaise
McCormick Salad Supreme Seasoning
salt and freshly ground black pepper
4 baby green Vidalia Onions, chopped
bacon bits

Spread 1 tablespoon of mayonnaise around the inside of a large bowl. Mix remaining mayonnaise and sour cream together.

To assemble: place a layer of potatoes in the bowl; top with layers of cottage cheese, salt and pepper, salad seasoning, sour cream mixture and green onions in the order given.

Repeat layers and top with bacon bits. Chill before serving. (8 servings)

Note: This is inappropriate for a low-fat diet. If you substitute a non-fat sour cream or plain yogurt and a soy-based mayonnaise, the dish would be significantly lower in fat.

Bean and Onion Salad

2 cans dark red kidney beans, drained
1 can black beans, drained
1 green pepper, chopped
1 large Vidalia Onion, chopped
1/2 cup celery, chopped
2 large cloves garlic, finely chopped
1/2 cup olive oil
1/4 cup red wine vinegar
1/8 teaspoon paprika
1/2 teaspoon salt
1/4 teaspoon freshly ground black pepper

1 teaspoon honey
1 teaspoon Worcestershire sauce
1 tablespoon ketchup
2 drops of Tabasco sauce
3 tablespoons fresh, chopped parsley

Combine beans, green pepper, onion and celery in a large salad bowl. Place remaining ingredients in a small bowl and mix well.

Pour over beans and onions and toss. Chill and serve. (4 to 6 servings)

Note: This salad is a perfect picnic companion. Though best when served cold, it will not suffer if served at room temperature.

You may vary the beans with other seasonal or favored varieties.

Wilted Lettuce Salad

4 heads Bibb lettuce
4 slices of bacon
1/2 cup baby green Vidalia Onions, chopped
4 tablespoons white vinegar
3 tablespoons sugar
salt and pepper

Rinse lettuce, tear into bite-sized pieces and place in salad bowl. Top with green onions. Set aside.

Slowly fry bacon in heavy skillet (cast-iron works well) until crisp and brown. Remove bacon and drain on paper towels and set aside.

Reheat bacon drippings. (You should have about 3 tablespoons.)

Add sugar, salt and pepper. Remove from heat and carefully add vinegar.

To assemble: Pour hot vinegar mixture over lettuce and onions. Crumble bacon and sprinkle on top. Serve immediately. (6 servings)

Simple Salad for One

1 large piece lettuce, rinsed
3/4 cup chopped fresh tomato
1/2 cup low-fat cottage cheese
1 baby Vidalia Onion, thinly sliced
1 hard-cooked egg, chopped
1/4 cup canned tuna, drained
salt and pepper

Place lettuce on plate and arrange tomato over it. Add cottage cheese and top with onion, egg, tuna, salt and pepper.

Serve with toast or a muffin.

Note: There's nothing complicated or exotic about this salad. It's refreshing, healthy, fairly low in fat and quite tasty.

Mary-Lou's Spinach Salad

1 pound fresh spinach, rinsed
1 clove garlic, peeled and halved
2 medium Vidalia Onions, thinly sliced and
  separated into rings
1 can Mandarin oranges, drained
  and chopped
1 small bunch watercress, rinsed and chopped
salt and pepper to taste
Italian dressing

Rinse spinach again; tear leaves into bite-sized pieces and place in a wooden salad bowl that has been rubbed with cut garlic.

Top spinach with onions, oranges, watercress and salt and pepper.

Dress with commercial Italian dressing or make your own. (6 servings)

Note: If you use a low-fat salad dressing, this is a low-fat, low-cholesterol treat.

Miss Hattie's Vidalia Onion and Potato Salad

6 medium potatoes, cooked, peeled and sliced
1 medium Vidalia Onion, thinly sliced and separated
  into rings
1 cup mayonnaise
1/2 cup buttermilk
1 1/2 teaspoons dried dill weed
1/2 teaspoon salt
1/4 teaspoon freshly ground black pepper

Gently mix onion rings and potatoes in large serving bowl. Combine mayonnaise, buttermilk, dill weed, salt and pepper in a small bowl and mix well. Combine mayonnaise mixture with potatoes and onions and mix well. If dressing seems too thick, thin it with more buttermilk. If it seems too thin, add more mayonnaise. Adjust seasonings. (6 servings)

Note: To lower fat and cholesterol, use a light or soy-based mayonnaise.

Vidalia Onion Salad

2 cups thinly sliced Vidalia Onions
1 head of lettuce (iceberg, romaine or combination),
  torn into bite-sized pieces
8 hard-cooked eggs, sliced

Dressing:
  1/2 cup prepared mustard
  1/2 cup mayonnaise
  salt to taste
  1/8 teaspoon lemon-pepper seasoning
  2 teaspoons white vinegar
In a separate bowl, mix dressing ingredients.

To assemble: make layers of lettuce, onions, eggs and dressing. Repeat, ending with dressing. Cover and chill for 2 hours. (8 generous servings) Good with steak and potatoes.

Soups

Potato and Vidalia Onion Soup

1/2 cup butter, divided
2 large Vidalia Onions, coarsely chopped
2 medium potatoes, quartered
water
1/2 cup cream
3 tablespoons chopped baby Vidalia Onions
salt and pepper to taste

Sauté large onions in a Dutch oven in 1/4 cup butter until limp and tender. Add potatoes and enough water to barely cover. Bring to a boil, turn down heat and simmer until potatoes are tender, about 30 minutes. Remove from heat, and pour off about half the water. Pour potatoes with remaining water into blender, food processor or food mill and puree until smooth.

Return to saucepan, add 1/4 cup butter, cream and salt and pepper to taste. Just before serving, add freshly chopped baby Vidalia Onions.

Note: Do not allow soup to boil or the cream will curdle. Serve with hot corn bread, fresh green salad and brownies for dessert.

Potato and Vidalia Onion Soup, Option Two

This version of Potato and Vidalia Onion Soup is designed for those who are concerned about cholesterol and fat. Naturally, if you are on a strict heart-healthy diet, you should check with your nutritionist or doctor before adding or subtracting new foods.

4 medium potatoes, peeled and sliced
2 large Vidalia Onions, coarsely chopped
1 large carrot, chopped
2 stalks of celery, chopped
1/4 cup safflower oil
2 packets low-sodium chicken bouillon, prepared
  according to package directions
1 cup undiluted, evaporated skim milk
3 tablespoons freshly chopped parsley

Sauté vegetables in Dutch oven in oil until onions are limp. Cover with low-sodium bouillon (about 2 cups). Bring to a boil, turn down and simmer about 30 minutes or until vegetables are tender.

Remove from heat and pour into blender, food processor or food mill and puree until smooth. (You will probably have to do this in batches.) Pour smooth soup back into Dutch oven and add milk. Heat and add parsley just before serving.

Red Beans and Rice

1 pound dried red beans
1 large Vidalia Onion, chopped
1/4 pound (approximately) smoked ham hock
freshly ground black pepper
2-3 drops Tabasco sauce
3 cups cooked rice

Soak beans overnight. In the morning, drain and place them in a slow cooker with just enough fresh water to cover.

Add remaining ingredients except rice. Cover and cook on low for about 8 hours. Serve over hot rice. (4 servings)

Note: This is a simple version of a traditional New Orleans dish, which is also occasionally called Limpin' Susan for reasons everyone has long since forgotten.

Mother's Chicken Soup

1 large chicken
4 whole peppercorns
2 whole cloves
1 bay leaf
1/2 cup celery, chopped
2 large carrots, peeled and chopped
1 jumbo Vidalia Onion, chopped
2/3 cup raw, brown rice
1/2 cup frozen peas
1 teaspoon poultry seasoning
1/4 cup fresh parsley, chopped
salt and freshly ground black
    pepper to taste

Cover chicken with water in heavy Dutch oven. Bring to a boil. Skim off fat and scum. Add peppercorns, whole cloves and bay leaf.

Cover, turn down heat and simmer for 30 minutes. Turn chicken over and simmer another 30 minutes or until very tender. Remove chicken from pot and place in colander over sink to cool. Also, remove pot from burner and allow broth to cool.

Discard any fat that rises to the top; discard peppercorns and bay leaf as well. Debone chicken, discard bones, fat and skin, chop meat into bite-sized pieces and place back in the pot of broth.

Add all other ingredients. Bring to a boil. Turn down to a simmer, cover and cook for about 1 hour or until rice is done and vegetables are tender.

If the soup seems too thick, add water. If it's too thin, either add another 1/3 cup of raw brown rice (remembering that it takes almost 45 minutes to cook) or boil soup down. (6 to 8 servings)

Note: You may cut much of the fat in this dish by removing the skin and any obvious fat deposits from the chicken before cooking. Instead of beginning with a whole chicken, some prefer to make the soup from a leftover chicken carcass or perhaps from a collection of backs and wings that have accumulated in the freezer.

Vidalia Onion Borscht

1 pound lean stewing beef, cut into bite-sized pieces
9 cups water
1-2 pounds cabbage
6 fresh beets, washed and peeled
2 carrots, chopped
3 jumbo Vidalia Onions, chopped
1 6-ounce can tomato paste
1 can whole tomatoes or four fresh tomatoes, halved
salt to taste
1/4-1/2 teaspoon white pepper
1/2 teaspoon celery salt
1 bay leaf
6 allspice seeds
juice of 1 large lemon
2 tablespoons sugar

Place beef in large soup kettle with 9 cups of water. Bring to boil, turn down to simmer and cook until beef is almost tender. In the meantime, shred all vegetables except tomatoes in a food processor.

When beef is almost done, add cabbage, beets, carrots and onions to the kettle and simmer for about 30 minutes or until vegetables are tender. Add tomatoes, tomato paste and seasonings and cook for 10 more minutes. Then add lemon juice and sugar and continue cooking another 5 minutes. (6 to 8 servings)

Note: Soup may be served as is, or it may be served over peeled, boiled potatoes that have been cooked separately. This is an excellent recipe for those on a low-fat diet. Serve with coarse black bread for a complete Russian taste treat ... and lots of fiber.

Hoppin' John

1 pound dried black-eyed peas
8 slices bacon, diced
1 cup Vidalia Onion, finely chopped
1 large clove garlic, minced
1/4-1/2 teaspoon Tabasco sauce
1/8 teaspoon dried thyme
1/8 teaspoon dried rosemary
1/2 teaspoon salt
1/4 teaspoon freshly ground black pepper
3-4 cups cooked rice, cooked according to
   directions on package

Soak peas overnight. Place bacon in a large pot and fry over low flame until almost all the fat is rendered. Remove bacon and drain on paper towels.

Add chopped onion to bacon grease and sauté until onion is limp. Scrape onion with drippings into slow cooker.

Add set-aside bacon and other ingredients. Stir and barely cover with water.

Cook on low setting for about 8 hours. Serve over hot rice. (6 to 8 servings)

Folklore says that eating Hoppin' John on Jan. 1 will assure you of good luck throughout the year. Hoppin' John should be served with lots of collards and fresh corn bread.

Note: To cut the fat and cholesterol, leave out bacon and sauté onion in salad oil.

Cream of Onion Soup

2 medium Vidalia Onions, finely chopped
1/4 cup butter
1/2 cup flour
1 can clear chicken broth
chicken broth can of warm milk
1 1/2 cups warm water

1/2 teaspoon thyme
2 bay leaves
1/2 teaspoon salt
1/2 cup finely chopped peanuts

Sauté onions in butter until tender. Mix flour and chicken broth until smooth and add to onion mixture. Cook over medium-high heat, stirring constantly, for about 2 minutes.

Add milk and water and continue stirring until thick and smooth. Add other ingredients, turn heat to low and continue cooking for about 20 minutes, stirring occasionally. Do not let soup boil, or it will curdle.

Note: If you substitute vegetable oil for butter, skim milk for regular milk and eliminate the peanuts, this recipe should be suitable for those on a low-fat diet.

Broccoli-Vidalia Onion Soup

1 medium Vidalia Onion, chopped
2 tablespoons butter
2 8-ounce packages cream cheese, cut into
   1-inch cubes
2 cups milk
2 chicken bouillon cubes
1 1/2 cups boiling water
1 10-ounce package frozen chopped broccoli,
   cooked and drained
1 teaspoon lemon juice
salt and freshly ground black pepper to taste

Sauté onion in butter in heavy, large saucepan until the onion is tender. Add cream cheese and milk; stir over low heat until cheese melts.

Dissolve bouillon in boiling water and add to cream cheese mixture. Stir in broccoli, lemon juice, salt and pepper and heat thoroughly. Do not boil.

Note: See Option Two for low-fat, low-cholesterol version.

Broccoli-Vidalia Onion Soup — Option Two

1 medium Vidalia Onion, chopped
2 tablespoons vegetable oil
2 8-ounce packages light cream cheese
2 cups skim milk
2 low-sodium chicken bouillon cubes
1 1/2 cups boiling water
1 16-ounce package frozen broccoli cuts, cooked
   and drained according to package directions
1 tablespoon lemon juice
salt and freshly ground black pepper
Prepare as directed above.

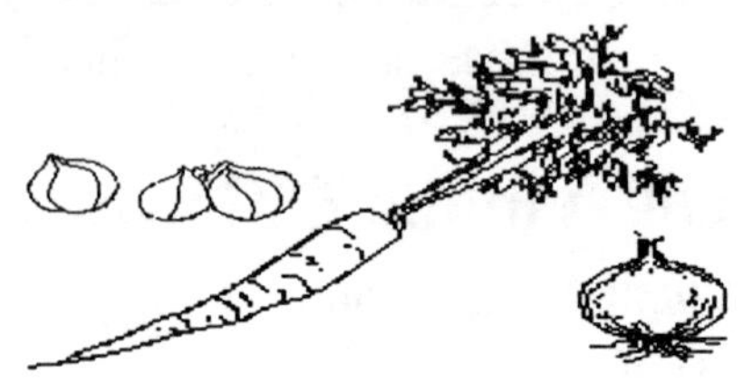

Lentil Soup

1 cup lentils
4 cups water
1/2 cup Vidalia Onion, chopped
1/2 cup celery, chopped
1/2 cup carrots, chopped
1 bay leaf
1 large clove garlic, minced
1/2 teaspoon salt
1/4 teaspoon freshly ground
   black pepper
1/2 teaspoon dried thyme
1 lemon, sliced (optional)
1 can Vienna sausages, chopped (optional)

Rinse lentils and place them in a Dutch oven with the
water. Add vegetables and spices. Bring soup to a boil,

lower heat, cover and simmer for about an hour or until vegetables are tender.

Check occasionally and if soup is too dry, add water. Five minutes before serving, add sausages and lemon slices, if you wish. (4 servings)

Note: Lentils are wonderful for cooks with busy schedules because the beans do not have to be soaked prior to use and because they cook up so quickly. Serve with corn bread, a green salad and apple pie for a filling, satisfying meal.

Lentil soup minus the sausages is a marvelous low-fat dish.

Kansas City Chili Topped With Vidalia Onions

1 pound ground beef
1 tablespoon oil
2 cloves garlic, mashed
2 cans dark red kidney beans with liquid
1 8-ounce can tomato sauce
1 6-ounce can tomato paste
1-3 teaspoons chili powder
1/2 teaspoon salt
1/4 teaspoon pepper
1/4 teaspoon sugar
1/4 teaspoon Tabasco sauce
1 small Vidalia Onion, finely chopped
vinegar

Sauté beef and garlic in oil until red disappears. Drain off fat. Add beans, tomato sauce, tomato paste, spices and Tabasco sauce.

Simmer for 30 minutes, stirring frequently. Divide into 4 large, soup bowls and top each bowl with a tablespoon of raw onion and vinegar. Serve with soda crackers. (4 servings)

Traditional French Onion Soup

6 cups thinly sliced Vidalia Onions
4 tablespoons butter
2 tablespoons oil
1 teaspoon salt
1/2 teaspoon sugar
3 tablespoons flour
2 quarts canned beef bouillon, boiling
1/2 cup dry white wine
salt and pepper
12-16 1-inch-thick slices of hard-toasted
   French bread
1/4 cup Swiss cheese cut into thin slivers
1 tablespoon grated Vidalia Onion
1 1/2 cups freshly grated Parmesan cheese
1 tablespoon olive oil

Slowly cook onions in butter and oil in large, heavy, covered saucepan for 15 minutes.

Uncover, raise the heat to medium and stir in salt and sugar.

Cook for about 35 minutes, stirring frequently, until onions are golden brown. Sprinkle in flour and stir for 2 minutes.

Add boiling bouillon all at once and stir until slightly thickened and smooth. Add wine and salt and pepper to taste. Simmer partially covered for 30 minutes, skimming occasionally.

Preheat oven to 325 degrees. Bring soup to a boil and pour into individual ovenproof soup bowls or a large tureen.

Stir in slivered cheese and raw onion. Float toast rounds on top of the soup and sprinkle with grated cheese. Drizzle with oil and bake for 20 minutes.

Run it under the broiler for a few seconds to brown the top and serve immediately. (6 to 8 servings)

Three-Meat and Onion Stew

1 pound lean stew beef, cut into
   bite-sized pieces
1/2 pound skinned and boned chicken,
   cut into bite-sized pieces
1/2 pound lean pork, cut into
   bite-sized pieces
1 teaspoon dried thyme
1/2 teaspoon salt
1/4 teaspoon cayenne pepper
1/4 teaspoon freshly ground black pepper
1/4 cup cooking oil (not olive)
2 jumbo Vidalia Onions, chopped
1 large green pepper, chopped
2 6-ounce cans tomato paste
1/2 cup red cooking wine

Combine cut-up meat and season with half the salt, peppers and thyme. Set aside for several minutes to allow the seasonings to penetrate the meat.

Heat oil in heavy Dutch oven and brown meat. Remove meat to paper towels to drain. Reheat oil and add onions, green pepper and remaining spices.

Sauté until limp. Add tomato paste, the set-aside meat and cooking wine. Bring to a boil, cover and turn heat down. Simmer 1 1/2 hours or until meat is tender. Check occasionally and if stew is too dry, add more wine or water. Serve over rice or couscous. (4 to 6 servings)

Note: After browning the meat and sautéing the vegetables, you could combine all the ingredients in a slow cooker and cook on low for about 8 hours.

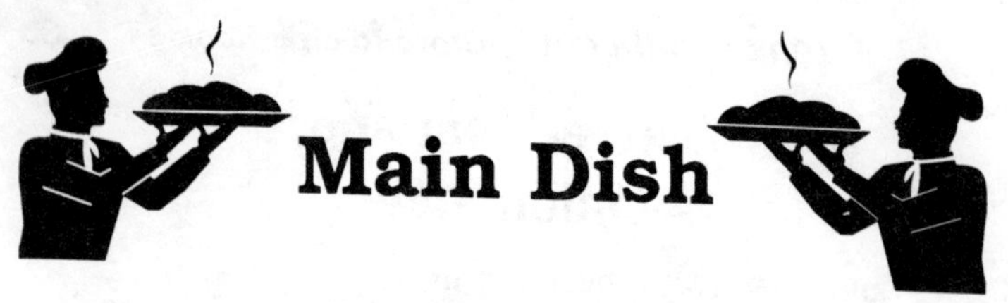# Main Dish

Chicken Dinner Casserole

1 10-ounce package frozen broccoli cuts
1/3 cup chopped Vidalia Onion
1/2 cup sliced mushrooms
2 tablespoons cooking oil
1 cup cheddar cheese, grated
2 eggs, slightly beaten
1/2 cup mayonnaise
1 cup water
1 cup cooked rice
6 chicken breasts, skinned and boned
3 tablespoons cooking oil
paprika

Cook broccoli according to package directions. Drain and set aside. Sauté onions and mushrooms in 2 tablespoons cooking oil until limp. Drain and combine with broccoli. Set aside.

Combine cheese, eggs, mayonnaise, water and rice. Set aside.

Rinse chicken breasts thoroughly in cold water and pat dry. Brown in 3 tablespoons cooking oil, adding more oil if necessary.

To assemble: Combine broccoli mixture with cheese mixture and pour into greased, shallow baking pan.

Place chicken breasts on top and sprinkle with paprika. Bake uncovered in a 350-degree oven for 45 minutes. (6 servings)

Note: You may cut fat and cholesterol from this recipe with the following substitutions: light, skim milk cheese for cheddar; 4 ounces of Second Nature egg substitute for the 2 eggs; light mayonnaise for regular mayonnaise; and non-stick cooking spray for greasing your baking dish.

Chicken Sopa

1 chicken
1 cup Vidalia Onion, chopped
2 tablespoons cooking oil
1 can cream of mushroom soup, undiluted
1 cup chicken broth
1/2 - 1 can Rotel tomatoes
2 cups medium sharp cheddar
  cheese, grated
10 (approximately) soft flour tortillas

Remove skin and fat from chicken. Place bird in large pot and cover with water. Bring to a boil, lower heat, cover and simmer for about 30 minutes.

Turn chicken over and cook another 30 minutes or until very tender. Remove chicken. Save 1 cup of the broth and strain the remaining broth for another use. When chicken is cool enough to handle, debone it and cut the meat into bite-sized pieces; discard fat and bones. This could all be done the day before.

Sauté Vidalia Onion in oil until limp and transparent. Scrape into bowl and combine with soup, broth and Rotel tomatoes.

To assemble: Grease a large rectangular casserole dish and line it with half the tortillas. Next, add half the soup and onion mixture.

Top with half the chicken and half the cheese. Repeat layers. Bake in a preheated 350-degree oven for about 1 hour. (8 servings)

Note: Rotel tomatoes are usually found among other brands of canned tomatoes. If your grocery does not carry Rotel tomatoes, substitute regular canned tomatoes and a 4-ounce can of chopped green chilies.

Liver and Vidalia Onions

1 pound beef or calf's liver, sliced
  1/2 - 3/4 inch thick
2 jumbo Vidalia Onions, thinly sliced and
  separated into rings
1/4 cup all-purpose flour
1/2 teaspoon salt
1/4 teaspoon freshly ground black pepper
1/4 cup cooking oil (not olive)
1/4 cup water

Heat half of the oil in a large, heavy skillet and sauté onions until almost tender. Remove onions to paper towels and set aside. Add remaining oil and reheat skillet.

While skillet is reheating, combine flour, salt and pepper in a plastic food-storage bag. Add liver and shake until well-coated. Sauté liver until brown on both sides. Add set-aside onion and water to skillet. Cover, turn heat to medium and cook about 3 minutes or until liver is dry around the edges and slightly pink in the middle. Do not overcook. (4 servings)

Cheesy Onion Pie

4 cups Vidalia Onion, thinly sliced and
  separated into rings
1 cup water
3 eggs, slightly beaten
1/2 teaspoon salt
1/4 teaspoon Tabasco sauce
1/2 cup cream
1 unbaked 9-inch pie shell
1 1/2 cups shredded sharp cheddar cheese

Preheat oven to 425 degrees. In a large saucepan, combine onions and water. Parboil for about 5 minutes. Drain.

Combine eggs, cream, Tabasco and salt in small bowl. Blend well.

Place half the onions in pie shell, then half the cheese. Repeat. Pour egg mixture over filling. Bake 15 minutes. Reduce oven temperature to 350 degrees and bake 25 minutes longer. Allow to stand for about 15 minutes before cutting and serving. (6 servings)

Note: For a slightly different taste, fry four slices of bacon and crumble them over the first onion layer. This dish is not appropriate for a low-fat, low-cholesterol diet. Some of the fat could be cut by using an egg substitute, a light cheese for the cheddar, and non-fat, evaporated skim milk for the cream.

Smothered Chicken With Vidalia Onions

1 chicken, cut up (about 3 pounds)
1/3 cup flour
1/2 teaspoon salt
1/8 teaspoon pepper
1/4 cup shortening or oil (not olive)
1 package dried chicken noodle soup mix
1 medium Vidalia Onion, sliced thinly and
   separated into rings
1 cup evaporated milk
1 cup water

Combine flour, salt and pepper in a plastic food-storage bag. Add chicken and shake to coat well. In a 10-inch skillet, melt shortening or oil and brown chicken. Drain off fat and sprinkle soup mix and onions over chicken in skillet. Mix together milk and water and add to skillet. Cover and cook over low heat about 30 minutes or until chicken is done. If dish seems too dry, add more liquid. Serve over rice. (4 to 6 servings)

Note: To cut fat from this dish, substitute skinned chicken breasts for the whole chicken and evaporated skim milk for regular evaporated milk.

Hearty Meat and Vidalia Onion Pie

First layer:
   1 can biscuits

Second layer:
   1 pound ground beef
   1/4 teaspoon Tabasco sauce
   1 medium Vidalia Onion, chopped
   1 ounce dried mushrooms
   2 eggs
   1/2 teaspoon Italian seasoning
   1 tablespoon chopped fresh parsley
   1/2 teaspoon salt
   1/4 teaspoon oregano
   1/2 teaspoon freshly ground black pepper

Third layer:
   1 cup Swiss cheese, grated
   1 cup sharp cheddar cheese, grated
   3 eggs
   1/2 cup sour cream
   1/2 cup half and half

First layer: Make a pie shell out of the canned biscuits.

Second layer: Soak mushrooms in 1/2 cup water. Set aside. Sauté meat and onions in small amount of oil until red disappears on the meat and the onions are limp. Drain off excess fat and add set-aside mushrooms with liquid and seasonings. Mix well.

Remove from heat and add 2 eggs. Mix well and pour on top of biscuit layer

Third layer: Mix next five ingredients and spread over meat layer. Bake in a 350-degree oven for about 30 minutes or until brown. (4 to 6 servings)

Note: Those who are concerned about fat and cholesterol may want to make the following substitutions: 1/4 cup egg substitute (found alongside fresh eggs in the dairy case) for every egg called for in the recipe; part skim milk cheddar and Swiss for the cheeses, light sour cream or non-fat plain yogurt for sour cream, and evaporated skim milk for the half and half.

Hot Chicken Pasta Stir Fry

If you can't afford a world cruise with its variable ethnic cuisine, just try this recipe. It seems to include a dash of Tex-Mex, Chinese, Italian and traditional North American.

**1 1/2 cups wheel-shaped pasta, cooked
  and drained
2-3 tablespoons vegetable oil
1 medium Vidalia Onion, sliced
2 whole, boned chicken breasts, washed, dried
  and cut into 1/2-inch cubes
2 small green peppers, cut into strips
1/2 teaspoon ground cumin
1/2 teaspoon cayenne
1 8-ounce can whole kernel corn, drained
1 10-ounce can Rotel tomatoes, undrained
2 tablespoons cornstarch
1 cup grated sharp cheddar cheese**

Cook pasta according to package directions. Drain and set aside.

Heat oil in wok or large skillet over high heat. Add chicken and stir fry until pieces turn white. Add green peppers, onion, cumin and cayenne. Stir fry for 3 minutes. Add additional oil if necessary.

Stir in drained corn, pasta and salt. Cover and cook 2 minutes. Drain tomatoes, reserving liquid. Add tomatoes with chilies to cooked mixture.

Mix cornstarch with half of the reserved tomato liquid. (Discard other half.) Add cornstarch mixture to wok, bring to boil, stirring constantly until thickened. Reduce heat and sprinkle cheese on top. Cover and cook about 2 minutes or until cheese melts. (4 servings)

Regal Onion Delight

2 strips of bacon
1 carrot, thinly sliced
6 small, whole Vidalia Onions, cut in
   thick slices
1/2 cup fresh mushrooms, sliced
2 tablespoons margarine
1/2 teaspoon salt
1/2 teaspoon paprika
2 tablespoons cornstarch
1/2 cup water
1/2 cup evaporated milk

Fry bacon until crisp and drain on paper towels. Slice carrot thinly.

Place sliced carrots, onions and mushrooms in medium-sized saucepan, sprinkle with paprika and just barely cover with water. Cook over medium heat until tender (about 10-15 minutes).

Adjust heat to lowest setting and add margarine. Blend cornstarch with the 1/2 cup water and add to saucepan, stirring gently but constantly.

When mixture has thickened — about 2 minutes — remove from heat and add evaporated milk. Crumble bacon on top and serve with hot, fluffy rice.

Note: To cut fat and cholesterol, leave out bacon and use evaporated skim milk.

Onion, Meat and Potato Casserole

6 large Vidalia Onions, peeled and thinly sliced
6 large white potatoes, peeled and thinly sliced
2 cans condensed cream of mushroom soup
4 tablespoons oil
1/2 teaspoon salt
1/4 teaspoon freshly ground black pepper
2 pounds lean ground beef

Brown meat in hot oil; drain off fat and add salt and pepper.

Grease large casserole dish and make alternate layers of onions, potatoes and meat. Pour mushroom soup on top and bake at 350 degrees for 45 minutes. (8 generous servings)

Note: This casserole is perfect for the meat and potatoes gang.

Fake Soufflé

2-3 jumbo Vidalia Onions
6 ounces Italian bread, torn into chunks
1/2 cup butter, melted
1 teaspoon dried thyme
1 1/4 cup grated Swiss cheese
2 cups undiluted, evaporated skim milk
3 eggs
1/2 teaspoon salt
1/4 teaspoon coarsely ground black pepper
Preheat oven to 350 degrees.

Place chunks of bread in a greased 1 1/2-quart casserole or soufflé dish. Set aside. Slice onions thinly and sauté them in the melted butter until limp. Scrape onions and butter over bread chunks in soufflé dish. Add salt, pepper and thyme.

Beat eggs and evaporated milk together until frothy. Pour over mixture in soufflé dish. Press down to make sure bread is soaking up milk. Sprinkle cheese over the top and bake 45 minutes or until knife inserted in the center comes out clean.

This is not as light as a traditional soufflé, but it's easy to prepare and reheats well. (6 servings)

Note: For a richer dish, substitute cream for evaporated skim milk. Or, for a lighter dish, substitute a light cheese food in place of the Swiss cheese and an egg substitute for at least two of the eggs.

Vidalia Onion Pork Chops
and Spanish Rice

1 tablespoon cooking oil (not olive)
4 1-inch-thick loin pork chops
4 1-inch-thick slices Vidalia Onion
1/2 teaspoon dried oregano
1/2 teaspoon dried basil
1/2 teaspoon dried thyme
1/2 teaspoon salt
1/8 teaspoon freshly ground black pepper
3/4 cup chopped green pepper
2 large cloves garlic, finely chopped
1-2 teaspoons chili powder
1/8 teaspoon cayenne pepper
12 ounces tomato sauce
1 cup raw white rice
1 can undiluted chicken broth

Heat oil in heavy skillet and brown chops. Remove and place in a greased, shallow casserole dish just large enough to hold them. Sprinkle chops with oregano, basil, thyme, salt and freshly ground black pepper. Set aside.

Reheat skillet and sauté green pepper and garlic in pork chop drippings. When pepper begins to lose its bright green color, add rice, tomato sauce, cayenne, chili powder and chicken broth. Stir well and remove from heat.

To assemble: Place one onion slice on top of each chop. If desired, sprinkle with more cayenne, salt and pepper or chili powder.

Pour tomato-rice sauce over all and cover casserole securely. Bake in a preheated 350-degree oven for about 45 minutes or until chops and rice are tender. Check casserole several times and stir. If it seems too dry, add water or chicken broth. (4 servings)

Note: This dish is a full meal. Just add a fresh fruit salad and homemade cookies and ice cream for dessert.

Sausage-Stuffed Main Dish Onions

4 large Vidalia Onions
1/2 pound hot pork sausage
1/4 cup chopped green pepper
1 egg, beaten
1 cup cooked rice
1/2 cup soft bread crumbs
1/2 teaspoon dried whole oregano
2 tablespoons chopped fresh parsley
2 tablespoons butter
1 teaspoon paprika

Preheat oven to 400 degrees.

Peel onions and cut a slice from the top. Cook onions in boiling salted water 12 minutes or until tender, but not mushy. Cool.

Remove the centers of the onions, leaving shells intact. Chop onion centers and reserve 1/2 cup.

Sauté sausage, stirring to crumble; remove browned sausage with slotted spoon to paper towels to drain. Sauté green pepper and reserved onion in pan drippings until tender.

Combine sausage, pepper, reserve onion, egg, rice, bread crumbs, oregano and parsley. Mix lightly and fill onion shells.

Place filled shells in shallow baking pan that is just large enough to hold them. Add 1/2 cup hot water. Brush onions with butter and sprinkle with paprika. Cover pan and bake for 15 minutes. Uncover and bake an additional 5 minutes. (4 servings)

Note: To dress up this dish, try topping onions with a medium white sauce that has been flavored with a dash of nutmeg.

Serve with sliced tomatoes lightly dressed with olive oil and oregano and crisp-tender green beans. This recipe is inappropriate for a low-fat, low-cholesterol diet.

Vidalia Onion Foil Meal or Scout Camp Special

1 thick, lean ground beef patty per person
1 thick slice Idaho potato per person
1 thick slice jumbo Vidalia Onion per person
butter or margarine
salt and pepper
1 teaspoon Worcestershire sauce per
**   person (optional)**

On a piece of heavily buttered foil, place 1 beef patty and top it with potato and onion slices. Place dots of butter or margarine on top of the pile and sprinkle with Worcestershire sauce, if desired. Add salt and pepper to taste. Twist foil together at top to enclose package. Make sure there are no leaks or holes.

Place package in ovenproof dish and bake at 350 degrees for about 1 hour and 20 minutes.

Note: This is a traditional scout camp meal upgraded for the kitchen. For camping, place packages over hot coals.

Catchy Catfish

4 catfish fillets (about 1 1/2 pounds)
1/2 cup fresh parsley, chopped
1/2 cup baby green Vidalia Onions, chopped
1 teaspoon dried tarragon
1 teaspoon dried chervil
2 tablespoons fresh rosemary, chopped
2 tablespoons freshly squeezed lemon juice
1/4 cup grated Parmesan cheese
2 tablespoons olive oil

Spray a shallow casserole dish just large enough to hold fish in a single layer with a non-stick cooking spray. Place fish in a casserole dish and sprinkle with remaining ingredients in the order given. Bake in a preheated 350-degree oven for about 30 minutes or until fish flakes when pierced with a fork. Do not overbake.

Note: Different herbs may be substituted for those listed above. The important point is to have a mixture of fresh and dried. Remember, you need about three times as much of a fresh herb as a dried one. This recipe is excellent for those on a low-fat diet. Try it with Copper Pennies (see Side Dishes) and steamed broccoli for a colorful and tasty meal that is also healthy.

Winter Dinner

1 1/2 pounds stew beef, cut into bite-sized pieces
1 large Vidalia Onion, chopped
2 large cloves garlic, chopped
1/2 teaspoon salt
1/4 teaspoon freshly ground black pepper
1 cup smoke-flavored barbecue sauce
1/4 cup cooking sherry
1/2 cup beef bouillon
1 1-pound package frozen lima beans
4 medium-sized baking potatoes

Spray inside of slow cooker with a non-stick cooking spray. Place chopped onion and garlic in cooker. Add meat and sprinkle with salt and pepper. Add frozen beans.

Mix together barbecue sauce, sherry and bouillon. Pour over all and mix. Cook on low for about 8 hours.

Right before dinner, scrub potatoes and bake in a conventional oven or microwave until tender.

To assemble: Place one potato on each plate. Cut it into 4 pieces, salt and pepper each one, but do not remove peel. Top each potato with meat mixture.

Note: The slow cooker part of this dinner can be put together in less than 15 minutes in the morning before leaving for work. If you microwave your potatoes, your total kitchen time for this full meal would be less than half an hour! And it's healthy, too!

Sauerkraut, Sausage and Onion Casserole

1 1/2 cups sauerkraut, drained
1 pound Polish sausage (Kielbasa), quartered
2 large carrots, scraped and chopped
2 large potatoes, peeled and cut into
  2-inch chunks
3 slices of bacon
1 small Vidalia Onion, minced
salt and freshly ground black pepper

Place chopped carrots and potatoes in a medium-sized saucepan of boiling water. Bring water back to a boil and boil for 2 minutes. Drain and place vegetables on paper towels to dry.

Fry bacon in a heavy skillet. Remove bacon and drain on paper towels. Add onion to bacon drippings and sauté until limp.

Add carrots and potatoes and stir to coat with drippings. Remove skillet from heat and set aside.

Grease a large, shallow casserole dish and cover bottom with sauerkraut. Place onions, carrots and potatoes with drippings on top of the sauerkraut. Lightly salt and pepper the vegetables.

Place sausage on top of vegetables and sprinkle crumbled bacon over all.

Cover casserole and bake in a preheated 325-degree oven for about 30 minutes or until vegetables are fork tender and sausage is hot.

Serve with fresh green salad and fruit compote for dessert.

Note: This dish is inappropriate for a low-fat diet. Some of the fat can be cut by using turkey sausage, eliminating the bacon, and sautéing the onions in 2 tablespoons of cooking oil.

Comfort Casserole

1 large Vidalia Onion, chopped
2 tablespoons cooking oil
1 pound lean, ground beef
1/2 teaspoon salt
1/4 teaspoon freshly ground black pepper
1 1-pound can green beans, drained
1 can tomato soup, undiluted
3 medium-sized potatoes
1 tablespoon butter
2-4 tablespoons milk
1/2 cup grated cheddar cheese

Heat oil in large, heavy skillet and sauté onion until it is limp and transparent. Add ground beef and continue sautéing until the red disappears.

Remove from heat and drain well. Stir in tomato soup. Set mixture aside.

In the meantime, peel potatoes and chop them into pieces about the size of small eggs. Place in saucepan and just barely cover with water. Cook until potatoes are very tender. Drain well.

Place potatoes back in saucepan and add butter and milk. Beat with electric beater until fluffy. If necessary, add more milk.

To assemble: Grease large, rectangular casserole and pour in set-aside meat mixture. Place green beans on top of meat. Cover all with mashed potatoes and sprinkle cheese over all. Bake in a preheated 350-degree oven for about 25 minutes.

Note: This is inappropriate for a low-fat diet, but perfect for the "meat and potatoes" group. When someone mentions comfort food, I always think of this plain, but tasty and filling, casserole.

You may substitute instant potato flakes for the home-made mashed potatoes.

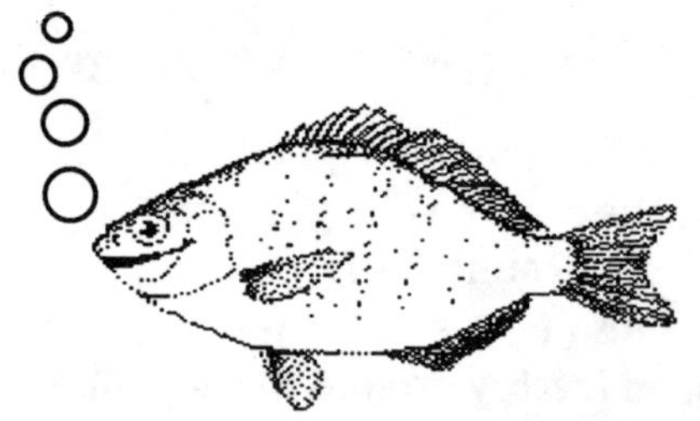

Baked Fish With Vidalia Onions Over Brown Rice

3 jumbo Vidalia Onions, sliced
2-4 tablespoons olive oil
1-2 pounds white fish fillets
1/2 cup cider vinegar
1 teaspoon ground cardamom
2 teaspoons turmeric
1 teaspoon chili powder
1/2 teaspoon cumin
3 large cloves garlic, crushed
1/2 teaspoon salt
1 6-ounce can tomato paste
1 cup of water
3 cups brown rice, cooked according to
   package instructions

Preheat oven to 350 degrees. Sauté onions in oil until limp. Set aside.

Place raw fish, cut into serving-sized pieces, in greased baking dish. Cover with onions. Combine all other ingredients, except rice, and mix well.

Pour over fish and bake 45 minutes to an hour or until fish flakes easily when pierced with a fork.

Place cooked rice on serving platter and pour fish with sauce and onion over all. (4 to 6 generous servings)

Note: You may use almost any kind of grain you wish in place of brown rice. Try serving it with couscous, for example. Also, this recipe is low in fat and cholesterol.

Colorful Veggie Pasta With Vidalia Onions

This unusual recipe is expensive and time consuming to make, but it is delicious when you're in the mood for something exotic.

- 2 red bell peppers
- 1 yellow bell pepper
- 12 medium-sized fresh mushrooms, sliced
- 1 6-ounce jar marinated artichoke hearts with liquid
- 1 medium Vidalia Onion, thinly sliced and separated into rings
- 2 dozen cherry tomatoes, halved
- 2 teaspoons dried basil
- 3-4 cloves garlic, minced
- 1/2 teaspoon salt
- 6 tablespoons olive oil
- 2 tablespoons Balsamic vinegar
- 15 oil-cured olives, pitted and chopped
- 1/2 pound spaghetti
- 1/2 cup freshly grated Parmesan cheese

Broil peppers until skin is black and blistered on all sides. Remove and place in brown, paper bag for five minutes.

When cool enough to handle, remove stem, seeds and skin and cut into strips and place in a large bowl. Add all other ingredients except spaghetti and Parmesan. Cover bowl and marinate at room temperature for several hours or overnight.

To assemble: Cook spaghetti according to directions on the package.

Heat veggies in microwave or heat gently in a large skillet over low heat, but do not cook them. Combine warm vegetables and pasta and serve immediately. Pass cheese separately. (4 servings)

Side Dishes

Vidalia Onions With Cheese Sauce

12 medium Vidalia Onions
1 teaspoon salt
4 tablespoons butter
4 tablespoons flour
2 cups boiling milk
paprika
2 hard-boiled eggs, finely chopped or grated
1 cup grated cheese
1/2 teaspoon Worcestershire sauce
fresh parsley

Peel onions and cook in boiling, salted water until tender. Drain and cool. Place onions in serving dish and keep warm.

In a heavy saucepan, melt butter and blend in flour. Cook over medium heat, stirring constantly, for about 2 minutes. Add boiling milk all at once and continue stirring and cooking until mixture is thick and smooth. Remove from heat and add grated cheese and Worcestershire sauce.

Pour cheese sauce over onions and garnish with eggs, parsley and paprika. Serve immediately. (8 to 10 servings)

Note: To cut cholesterol and fat, substitute oil for butter, skim milk for whole milk, and low-fat cheese for regular cheese. Eliminate yolk part of hard-boiled eggs.

Charlotte's Vidalia Onion Pudding

5 cups sliced onion
4 tablespoons butter
1/2 cup self-rising flour

salt and pepper to taste

4 cups grated, mild, white cheese

Preheat oven to 325 degrees. Place sliced onions in a saucepan and just barely cover with water. Bring to a boil. Remove from heat and drain. Set aside.

Melt butter in large, heavy skillet over medium-high heat. Combine salt and pepper with flour and mix into melted butter.

Cook, stirring constantly, for about 3 minutes. Remove from heat and mix roux (flour and butter mixture) with drained onions and 3 cups of cheese.

Pour into greased casserole dish (2-quart size) and sprinkle remaining cheese on top. Bake for 30 minutes. (6 servings)

Note: When you read this recipe, you will probably think that someone left out something. But when you try it, you will be pleasantly surprised. The finished dish tastes great. To cut fat and cholesterol, substitute a low-fat cheese and margarine for the butter. This is a good recipe for covered-dish dinners because it doesn't have to be served right out of the oven.

Onions and Carrots, Plain and Simple

1 cup carrots, diagonally sliced

1 Vidalia Onion, thinly sliced and separated into
  rings

1/4 teaspoon dry rosemary

1/4 teaspoon dry thyme

1 tablespoon fresh parsley, chopped

salt and pepper

Steam carrots and onions for about 15 minutes, depending on size and thickness of carrots, or until crisp tender. Place in serving dish and toss with other ingredients. (4 servings)

Note: This is an excellent low-fat dish.

Onion Mushroom Casserole

4-5 cups Vidalia Onions, peeled and cut
  into chunks
1/4 cup butter, melted
1/2 teaspoon salt
freshly ground black pepper
1 1/2 cups fresh mushrooms, sliced
1 3-ounce package cream cheese
3 tablespoons flour
1 1/2 cups milk
1/4 cup grated cheddar cheese
1/4 cup cracker crumbs

Combine onions with butter, mushrooms and salt. Simmer for 5 minutes in a sauté pan or large skillet. Add cream cheese. When melted, add flour and milk. Reheat. Turn into 1 1/2 or 2-quart greased casserole dish.

Mix grated cheese and cracker crumbs and sprinkle over the top. Bake in a preheated 400-degree oven for about 30 minutes. (5 servings)

Note: The fat and cholesterol in this recipe could be cut significantly by substituting vegetable oil for butter, skim milk for whole milk, low-fat cheese for cheddar, and light cream cheese for regular cream cheese.

Grilled Vidalia Onions

Peel and core one medium-sized onion per person. Place each on a square of tin foil and sprinkle with about 1 tablespoon Worcestershire sauce, salt and pepper and 2 teaspoons butter.

Wrap onion well in foil and place on grill, but not directly over coals. Grill until onions are fork tender. Serve with grilled meat and fresh garden salad with homemade peach ice cream for dessert.

Note: To cut grilling time, parboil onions for about 3 minutes after peeling and coring.

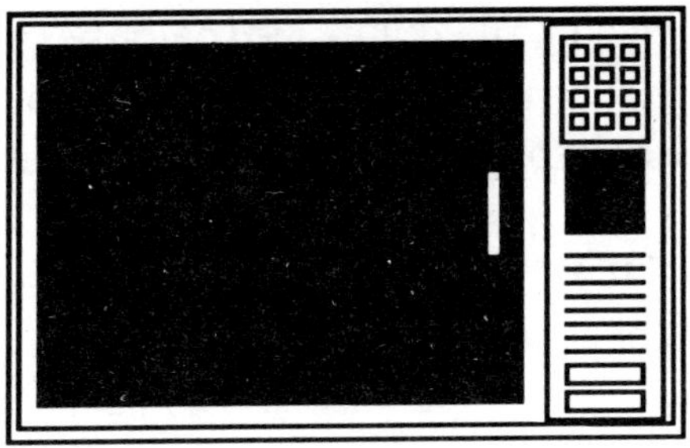

Stuffed Vidalia Onions
(Microwave)

1 large Vidalia Onion, sliced in thirds crosswise
1 tablespoon melted butter
1/8 teaspoon salt
1 cup dry herb bread stuffing
1/4 cup beef broth
1/4 teaspoon freshly ground black pepper

In a 1 1/2-quart casserole dish, place a piece of plastic wrap large enough to wrap stuffed onion.

In a medium-sized bowl, mix dry stuffing, beef broth, melted butter, salt and pepper. Mixture should be moist but not soggy.

Place bottom third of onion in the center of the plastic wrap. Top with slightly less than half of the stuffing; repeat with middle third of onion, reserving 1 tablespoon of the stuffing for the topping.

Take top of onion and cut a hole in the center just large enough for remaining stuffing. Place onion on top of the stack and fill with the tablespoon of stuffing. Pull up edges of plastic wrap and tie loosely with string. Microwave on high 6 minutes.

Let stand approximately 10 minutes. When done, onion should be fork tender.

Note: Larger onions will require longer cooking.

Baked Vidalia Onions

Peel and core one medium-sized onion per person and place in baking dish just large enough to hold them. Fill cores with 1 tablespoon margarine and 1 tablespoon soy sauce.

Cover and bake in preheated 350-degree oven for 45 minutes. Uncover and continue baking for another 15 minutes. Excellent and easy accompaniment to roast beef or roast pork.

Honey Onions

4 medium Vidalia Onions
1/2 cup hot water
2 tablespoons tomato juice
1 1/2 tablespoons honey
1/2 teaspoon salt
1/2 teaspoon paprika
1/4 teaspoon freshly ground black pepper

Preheat oven to 350 degrees. Peel onions and cut in half crosswise. Place onion halves, cut side up, in a 12x8x2-inch baking dish. Add 1/2 cup water to the pan. Combine remaining ingredients; stir well. Pour over onions and bake for 1 hour. Baste onions every 15 minutes. If mixture seems too dry, add water. (8 servings)

Note: This recipe is appropriate for those on a low-fat, low-cholesterol diet.

Scalloped Potatoes With Vidalia Onions

4 medium potatoes, peeled, cooked and sliced
2 medium Vidalia Onions, thinly sliced
1 cup evaporated milk mixed with 1 T. vinegar
1 cup commercial sour cream
1/4 cup fresh parsley, chopped

salt and pepper to taste
1 cup grated Cheddar cheese
Place one layer sliced, cooked potatoes in buttered casserole dish. Top with layer of onions, parsley, salt and pepper. Repeat layers one or more times.

Combine milk and vinegar with sour cream and pour over all. Bake in a preheated 350-degree oven for 30 minutes. Check occasionally and if casserole seems too dry, add more milk.

If you wish, sprinkle cheese over casserole the last 10 minutes of cooking time. (6 servings)

Note: To cut fat and cholesterol, use evaporated skim milk and substitute plain, non-fat yogurt for sour cream. Use a part-skim milk light cheese in place of the cheddar.

Onion Gravy

2-3 cups chopped baby Vidalia Onions
1/4 cup bacon drippings
4-5 tablespoons flour
1 cup water, approximately
Sauté onion in bacon drippings in heavy skillet over medium heat until onion is limp. Mix flour with water in small bowl until smooth. Pour mixture into skillet and continue cooking and stirring until thick and smooth. Salt and pepper to taste.

Spoon over rice, mashed potatoes, meat loaf, buttered noodles or toast and serve immediately.

Note: There really isn't a non-fat or cholesterol-conscious substitute for gravy. By definition, gravy is heavily laden with fat and calories. But then, wouldn't you be suspicious of a gravy that was good for you?

Vidalia Onion and Pepper Stir Fry

4 green bell peppers
1 jumbo Vidalia Onion, peeled, thinly sliced
and separated into rings
2 tablespoons vegetable oil
2 tablespoons soy sauce
1 tablespoon water

Cut peppers in half. Remove core and seeds. Slice into 1/2-inch-wide strips.

Heat oil in large, heavy skillet or wok until very hot, but not smoking. Add onions and peppers and stir fry for about 2 minutes.

Add soy sauce and water and continue stirring for about 3 minutes or until crisp-tender. (4 servings)

Note: To stir fry, use a long-handled fork or wooden spoon and stir vegetables constantly. Do not allow vegetables to remain on surface of skillet for more than a few seconds at a time, or they will burn.

This recipe is appropriate for those on a low-fat, low-cholesterol diet.

Squash Casserole With Onions

3 cups fresh squash, sliced (yellow crookneck works well)

2 eggs
1 tablespoon butter
2 cups Ritz crackers, crushed
1 medium Vidalia Onion, finely chopped
2 cups mild, grated cheese (Monterey Jack)
1 tablespoon milk
1 can cream of chicken soup, undiluted

Cook squash in small amount of boiling, salted water until tender, but not mushy. Drain well.

Mix squash with other ingredients and pour into a greased casserole dish.

Bake uncovered in a 350-degree oven for about 30 minutes or until brown on top. Goes nicely with grilled hamburgers.

Add a fresh tomato salad for a colorful and tasty summertime meal. (6 servings)

Note: This recipe is not appropriate for those on a low-fat, low-cholesterol diet.

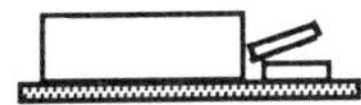

Vidalia Onion Casserole

5 jumbo Vidalia Onions
1 stick of butter or margarine
Parmesan cheese
1 stack crushed Ritz crackers

Peel and slice onions into thin rings. Sauté slowly in butter until limp. Pour half the onions into a greased 2-quart casserole.

Cover with Parmesan cheese and cracker crumbs. Repeat layers. Bake uncovered in a preheated 350-degree oven for about 25 minutes or until golden brown. (6 to 8 servings)

Note: This recipe is not appropriate for those on a low-fat, low-cholesterol diet.

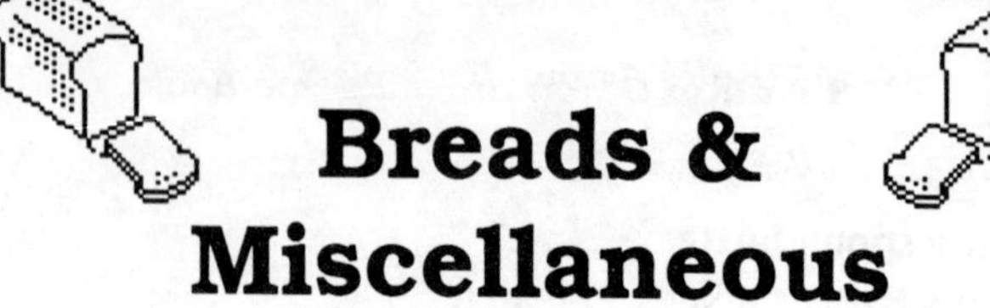

Breads & Miscellaneous

Stuffed Breakfast Onions

4 jumbo Vidalia Onions
4 small eggs
salt and pepper
paprika

Peel onions. Cut a thick slice from the top, and cut a thin slice from the bottom so the onions will stand. Drop onions in rapidly boiling salt water and boil for about 12 minutes or until tender, but not mushy. Remove onions from water and cool. When cool enough to handle, remove centers, leaving shells intact. Set aside centers for another use.

Salt and pepper inside shells. Break in egg. Carefully place shells in muffin tins or custard cups just large enough to hold them. Add 1 inch of hot water to each muffin tin or custard cup. Bake in a preheated 375-degree oven for 15 minutes or until eggs are set. Remove from oven and sprinkle with paprika.

Vidalia Onion Custard Bread

1 tablespoon vegetable oil
1/2 cup Vidalia Onions, thinly sliced
1 1/2 cups milk
1 egg, lightly beaten
1 1/2 cups buttermilk baking mix
1 cup grated sharp cheddar cheese, divided
1 tablespoon poppy seeds
2 tablespoons melted butter

Preheat oven to 400 degrees. Grease a 9-inch pie pan.

Heat 1 tablespoon oil in heavy, medium-sized skillet over medium-low heat. Add onions and cook, stirring occasionally, until golden brown, about 10 minutes. Set aside.

Combine milk and egg in medium-sized bowl. Blend in baking mix. Add onions and 1/2 cup cheese. Pour into prepared pan. Sprinkle with remaining 1/2 cup cheese and poppy seeds. Drizzle with butter.

Bake until golden brown, about 35 minutes. Cool slightly in pan. Cut into wedges and serve warm. (6 generous servings)

Sweet Vidalia Onion Buttered Hot Rolls

1 loaf frozen "Bake at Home" bread dough
Sweet Vidalia Onion Butter (See following recipe)

Place frozen loaf on greased baking sheet to thaw and rise at room temperature. Cover with waxed paper. Let dough rise to half the volume, about 2 1/2 hours.

Cut dough with sharp knife in pieces of 1 1/2-inch diameter. Form pieces into small balls, about the size of peach pits. Roll balls once in Sweet Vidalia Onion Butter. Place on baking sheet about 2 inches apart and cover with waxed paper. Let rolls rise until double in size, about 2 hours. Preheat oven to 375 degrees. Place rolls in oven and bake for 20 minutes or until golden brown.

Sweet Vidalia Onion Butter

1/2 cup butter, softened
1/4 cup finely chopped or grated Vidalia Onion
1/2 teaspoon salt
1 clove garlic, mashed
2 sprigs parsley, finely minced

Mix ingredients thoroughly and store in refrigerator. This will keep for several weeks.

Vidalia Onion Corn Bread

1/2 cup chopped Vidalia Onions
2 tablespoons butter
1 package corn muffin or corn bread mix
1/2 cup dairy sour cream
1/2 cup shredded sharp process Cheddar cheese

Sauté onion in butter until tender, but not brown. Set aside. Prepare mix according to package directions. Pour into a greased 8-inch square pan.

Sprinkle with set-aside onions. Mix sour cream and cheese and spoon over the top. Bake in a 400-degree oven for about 30 minutes or until bread begins to pull away from the sides of the pan and a toothpick inserted in the middle comes out clean. Let stand 30 minutes and cut into squares.

Vidalia Onion Supper Bread

1/2 cup chopped Vidalia Onions
2 tablespoons butter or oil
2 teaspoons bacon grease
1 egg, lightly beaten
3/4 cup milk
1 scant teaspoon sugar
1/2 teaspoon baking powder
1/2 teaspoon salt
1 cup cornmeal
1/2 cup flour
1/8 cup melted butter
1/2 cup dairy sour cream
1/2 cup sharp Cheddar cheese, grated

Sauté onion in 2 tablespoons butter or oil until limp. Set aside.

Pour bacon grease into an 8-inch square pan and place in a preheated 400-degree oven. Sift flour, sugar, baking powder, salt and cornmeal into a medium-sized bowl. In a small bowl, mix together egg, milk and 1/8 cup melted butter. Combine with dry ingredients and pour into heated pan.

Sprinkle sautéed onions on top of the batter. Mix together sour cream and cheese and spread over the onions.

Place back in 400-degree oven and bake about 25 minutes or until toothpick comes out clean, and corn bread begins to pull away from the sides of the pan.

Let stand about 10 minutes before cutting into squares and serving.

Vidalia Onion Supper Bread, Option Two

In this option, proceed as directed above. But, instead of topping the corn bread batter with the onions and sour cream/cheese mixture, fold onions and sour cream mixture into the batter. Bake as directed. The result will be the consistency of spoon bread.

Vidalia Onion Supper Bread, Option Three

If you are trying to cut down on fats and cholesterol, you may want to make the following substitutions:

* Safflower oil where the recipes call for butter, bacon grease or oil
* Two ounces of an egg substitute work as well as a whole egg
* Skim milk for whole milk
* Non-fat, plain yogurt for sour cream
* Light, skim milk cheese for regular cheese

You probably won't taste or notice the difference using any of these substitutions.

Hush Puppies

2 cups flour
1 1/2 cups yellow cornmeal
1/2 teaspoon salt
2 teaspoons baking powder
1 teaspoon sugar
2 eggs, lightly beaten
3/4 cup milk
1 small Vidalia Onion, finely chopped or grated
fat for frying

Fill a deep, heavy frying pan or cast-iron Dutch oven to within 2 inches of the rim with cooking oil, vegetable shortening or lard. Heat to 375 degrees on a deep-fat thermometer. If you don't have a deep-fat thermometer, drop a 1-inch cube of bread into the hot fat and count slowly to 60. If the bread browns in that minute, the fat is about 375 degrees and ready. If the fat isn't hot enough, your hush puppies will absorb too much oil and taste greasy. But, if the fat is too hot (smoking), your hush puppies will be underdone in the middle and burned on the outside.

In the meantime, combine flour, cornmeal, salt, baking powder and sugar in a medium-sized bowl. In a small bowl, mix together eggs, milk and onion. Combine the two mixtures and stir just until all is moist.

Drop by the teaspoonfuls into the hot fat and fry until lightly browned. Remove with a slotted spoon and drain briefly on paper towels. Fry just a few hush puppies at a time. Serve immediately.

Hush puppies are the Southern soul mate to "a mess of fried catfish." Complete your Southern, summer supper with corn on the cob, fresh green beans and juicy, sliced tomatoes. Top it all off with strawberry shortcake.